FIND YOUR INNER
SLOTH

FIND YOUR INNER
SLOTH

A JOURNAL CELEBRATING SLOW LIVING

OLIVER LUKE DELORIE

THUNDER BAY
P · R · E · S · S

San Diego, California

Thunder Bay Press
An imprint of Printers Row Publishing Group
10350 Barnes Canyon Road, Suite 100, San Diego, CA 92121
www.thunderbaybooks.com • mail@thunderbaybooks.com

Conceived, edited, and designed by Quarto Publishing plc,
6 Blundell Street, London, N7 9BH, UK.
QUAR.325447

Thunder Bay Press
Publisher: Peter Norton • Associate Publisher: Ana Parker
Acquisitions Editor: Kathryn Chipinka Dalby • Editor: Angela Garcia

Quarto Publishing
Deputy Art Director: Martina Calvio
Art Director: Gemma Wilson
Illustrators: Kuo Kang Chen, Olya Kamieshkova
Editor: Claire Waite Brown
Editorial Assistant: Charlene Fernandes
Publisher: Samantha Warrington

Additional illustrations:
aliaksei kruhlenia/Shutterstock.com; Anna Kulikova/Shutterstock.com; Auspicious/Shutterstock.com;
BoxerX/Shutterstock.com; brgfx/Shutterstock.com; Dimonika/Shutterstock.com;
Emila/Shutterstock.com; LenLis/Shutterstock.com; Maria Skrigan/Shutterstock.com;
Nadia Grapes/Shutterstock.com; NikhomTreeVector/Shutterstock.com;
Nikitina Olga/Shutterstock.com; norph/Shutterstock.com; Pikovit/Shutterstock.com;
Vallva/Shutterstock.com; WorkingPens/Shutterstock.com; WWWoronin/Shutterstock.com.

ISBN: 978-1-64517-457-8

Manufactured in China

24 23 22 21 20 1 2 3 4 5

CONTENTS

LOOKING AT LIFE FROM
UPSIDE DOWN

If sloths could scrutinize, they would do so upside down, but they don't have the energy. Suspended from the boughs of cecropia trees, their delightfully inverted view of the world surely lends itself to what we call context.

Leonardo da Vinci would look at a problem from at least three different angles, assuming his first way of looking at the issue was too biased and based on past experience to provide sufficient perspective. This inquisitive, innovative approach was what made him a genius.

If you have a problem you are finding difficult to solve—particularly if it involves conflict with another person—try looking at it from a different perspective and see if that helps.

Write down how you view a problem above the circle opposite, then note how the problem might appear from another person's point of view below the circle.

Do you have a favorite tree? Have you ever hugged it? How does it feel when you wrap your arms around it?

Color in the leaves and write a few words about how trees make you feel on the trunk.

HUG A TREE

All mommy, daddy, and baby sloths spend most of their lives hanging out in trees, doing mighty pull-ups and strenuous calisthenics all day long, even though they appear like lazy bums that do nothing all day. They've even got hanging out down to a science: they rarely move a muscle when they're dangling from a branch; they let their claws do all the heavy lifting.

Like hippies hunkering down in trees to protect the majestic plants they cherish from bulldozers, sloths are immune to weather. When they get wet, they simply drip-dry from a branch like undies pegged to a clothesline. Clothes pins are for backyards and the bumbling humans that inhabit them.

If you already enjoy being outdoors, you may have developed a deeper kinship with trees than with other humans. You are not alone. Flora and fauna are often more emotionally stable (and less demanding) than friends and family.

WHAT ARE YOU SMILING AT?

You know how sloths always look like they're smiling? That dark patch of fur below their mouths makes it look like they're having a grand old time, doesn't it?

According to psychologist Ronald E. Riggio, every time you smile you throw a feel-good party in your brain which activates nerve receptors that send instant messages packed with dopamine, endorphins, and serotonin. These same endorphins also act as a 100 percent organic pain reliever (without the negative side effects of synthetic concoctions attempting to do the same thing). Smiling is nature's antidepressant; it lowers your blood pressure and reduces stress, so you can be happier and healthier. Sign me up!

Conclusive conclusion: You don't have to learn therianthropy and shape-shift into a sloth; just smile more.

"A SMILE IS HAPPINESS YOU'LL FIND RIGHT UNDER YOUR NOSE."

Tom Wilson

Tick all the things below that make you smile.

- ☐ IT'S A BEAUTIFUL DAY
- ☐ YOU SPENT TIME WITH YOUR FRIENDS
- ☐ YOU LISTENED TO MUSIC YOU LIKE
- ☐ YOU ATE FOOD YOU ENJOY
- ☐ SOMEONE GAVE YOU A COMPLIMENT
- ☐ SOMEONE DID SOMETHING NICE FOR YOU TODAY
- ☐ YOU DID SOMETHING NICE FOR SOMEONE TODAY
- ☐ YOU HAD A GOOD LAUGH

- ☐ YOU SPENT TIME ENJOYING A HOBBY
- ☐ YOU FELT INSPIRED TODAY
- ☐ YOU FELT LOVED TODAY
- ☐ YOU READ A CHAPTER OF YOUR FAVORITE BOOK
- ☐ YOU HAVE EYES TO READ THIS!
- ☐ YOU ARE HEALTHY
- ☐ YOU HAVE EVERYTHING YOU NEED

SLEEP IN

According to those who study and profess what they've studied, we humans tend to benefit from 7–9 hours of sleep a night. Obviously, some of us sleep more, and some function quite well on less. As every human and every animal has unique needs, feel free to press the snooze button however many times you like.

Everyone knows sloths have it easy. But did you know the brown-throated specimen gets 15–18 hours of shut-eye a night? That's a lot of dreamtime. But if you were living in the neotropical zones of Central and South America where the weather is conducive most of the year, you could get away with an extra-long siesta too.

What do you think you would dream about if you were sleeping for three-quarters of your life? How could anything matter when you're snoozing under the covers, snug and cozy, for 18 hours a night?

In each cloud opposite, write down the dream you had the night before.

Date

Date

Date

Date

Look outside your window and describe what you see.
What is absolutely amazing about where you are right now?

BE HERE NOW

"Wherever you go, there you are," says Jon Kabat-Zinn. When you consider this, any sort of movement becomes a pointless exercise that will only distract you from seeing what is right in front of you. The grass ain't greener on the other side of the fence, nor on the other side of the pond. Your neighbor just went out, bought a watering can, filled it up, and watered their lawn every day.

Let everything be just the way it is. Tortoise-slow sloths seem to know this intuitively, so why don't we? They seem perfectly content if they make it the equivalent of half-way down a soccer field every day, so why do we fret and fuss about "not getting anywhere?" Dissatisfaction with "what is" squanders our time, money, and energy. Conservation of resources (along with present-moment awareness) is the key to success.

STAY COOL

While our internal temperature clocks in between 97.7 and 99.5 degrees Fahrenheit, our sedate sloth friends maintain a body temperature of 86–93 degrees. Due to the fact that they move so slow, it's easier for them to acclimate to their environment, regulate their internal temperature, and just live a simpler life.

These long-lost cousins of anteaters are able to achieve a serene state of homeostasis (the tendency to stabilize the elements of one's life) and remain cool, calm, and collected, unless of course they are being attacked. When that happens they scream!

How do you stay cool when the heat is on? How do you deal with conflict? From now on, ask yourself: What would a sloth do in this situation? Play it cool and take it easy; there's no need to lose your furry little head and have to fight back. Relax and you will ensure neither your—nor their—fluffy fur will fly.

Explain the methods you use to diffuse conflict and stay cool.

1 _____

2 _____

3 _____

HOT & BOTHERED

COOL & CALM

STAR(T)
FROM WHERE
YOU ARE

Sloths (like many life-forms) have come a long way. According to the San Diego Zoo, our furry friends roaming the wilds of North America 10,000 years ago were the size of elephants. Does that mean one day humans will be a fraction of the size we are now?

Regardless of how small and insignificant you may feel at times, just like the arboreal mammal we know and love, you can stretch and grow, take risks, and move at your own pace (or not). You can become anyone or anything you want in your humble, unhurried journey to wherever your heart leads you.

How does it feel to be wild? How does it feel to be tame? You, too, can enjoy the peace and quiet nestled in your tree-top nest. How peaceful a sloth's life must be.

SET YOURSELF SMALL GOALS THAT YOU CAN ACHIEVE AS YOU MOVE
SLOWLY THROUGH LIFE. WRITE ONE GOAL UNDER EACH STAR AS IT
SHRINKS IN SIZE TO REMIND YOU THAT NO MATTER HOW SMALL
YOU ARE, YOU CAN STILL FULFILL GREAT TRIUMPHS.

HONOR YOUR ANCESTORS

What if you knew you were related to superorder Xenarthra placental mammals who evolved on the continent of South America around 60 million years ago? Would you be at all curious about where you came from and/or how you ended up where you are?

As much as the people who raised you were well-intentioned, they are mere humans (and are thus limited to what they've learned in their relatively sloth-short lives, compared to the mind-boggling span of over 60 million years of evolution). Be patient; awareness of your place in the grand scheme of things usually doesn't manifest itself until you are almost an ancestor yourself, but when it does, connect with auntie/uncle/cousin/brother/sister/mother/father sloth.

When you (re)connect with family of all sloth shapes and sizes you may feel like the Grinch, who on Christmas morning realized the Whos didn't miss their Who grapes and surprises. When sloths of any age forgive their parents for dropping them from a branch that one time, they strengthen their family bond as a link in the generational chain. One small step for sloths, one giant step for relationships.

BUILD YOUR FAMILY TREE.

BREATHE
SLOW

Sloths can hold their breath underwater for up to 40 minutes. How do they do that? They slow their heart rate down to one-third of its normal BPM (beats per minute). Humans usually breathe in and out around 12–16 times per minute. Cut that in half (6 ins and outs per minute) and our brains and bodies not only relax, but our creative capacities also increase, which, once stirred, make it possible to solve more complicated problems and deal with stress in more constructive ways.

Only once you are in a serene state of tranquility will you receive the keys to the Kingdom (of Sloth), for studies show that learning to breathe slower can reduce stress, PTSD, panic attacks, and anxiety. Now plant the seeds of slow and harvest the benefits.

HOLDING THIS PAGE
CLOSE TO YOUR FACE,
BREATHE IN AS IF YOU
ARE SMELLING THE
FLOWER ON THE RIGHT...

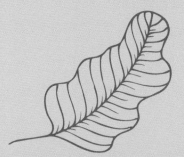

...THEN BREATHE OUT TRYING
TO BLOW THE LEAVES OFF
THE PAGE.

FIND YOUR
TREE

When you find your tree and your tribe, you are home. You probably don't have to go far (sloths don't). If home is where the heart is (and you've recently been wondering where all the love in your life has gone), find your tree home.

If ever you feel lost, believe it's possible that your people and your place are waiting for you just as much as (or more than) you want to find them.

People who think and feel and act like you do are to be cherished. The more you surround yourself with them, the more time will stand still (which is just how sloths like it).

Help your sloth find his home by completing the maze opposite.

HOME

START HERE

?

YOU ARE WHAT YOU EAT

A low-energy organic diet (including the green algae you find growing on your tummy) is known to be nourishing and nutritionally sufficient to sustain a life of leisure.

But if feasting on leaves isn't your idea of a Friday night out with friends, the food you choose to stuff yourself with has lasting effects on how energized you feel. If you often don't feel like doing anything, maybe becoming a folivore and eating mostly leaves will instead infuse your body with what it needs to sustain itself over the long term.

Over time, humans and animals adapted to whatever resources were immediately available. Fruits and vegetables were abundantly available once, so that is what most living creatures consumed. Nowadays we have access to anything we want, but are we creating the lives we want? You are what you eat. Are you a bacon cheeseburger or a kale salad?

Tick how many times this week you have eaten the leaves opposite.

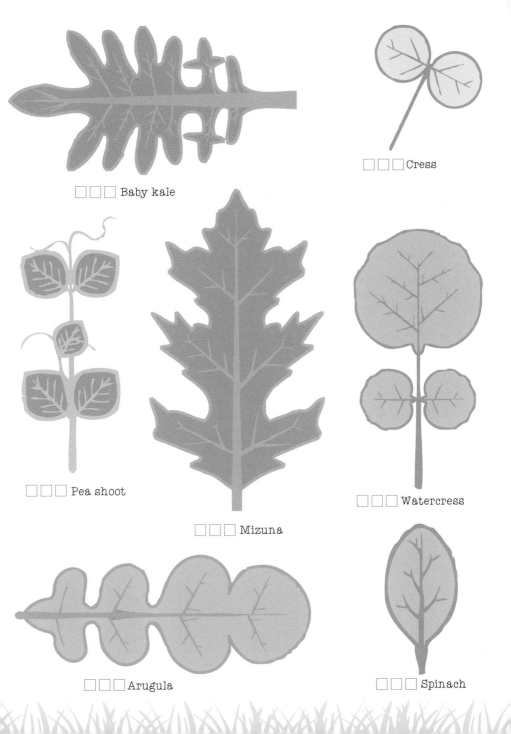

☐☐☐ Baby kale

☐☐☐ Cress

☐☐☐ Pea shoot

☐☐☐ Mizuna

☐☐☐ Watercress

☐☐☐ Arugula

☐☐☐ Spinach

GO SLOW

The more we put our pedal to the metal, the faster we wear out our brakes. Sloths (if you haven't noticed by now) are quite content in the slow lane of life. Do you ever wonder why people are so impatient to pass you? If so, going fast and furious is the last thing on your mind.

Another reason sloths are on slug-speed may be to catch a glimpse of the world going on around them. Perhaps they are keen observers of what's happening in the next tree over, or on the ground beneath them, or even as far off as over the horizon. They don't hear too well (they have tiny ears) but have great eyesight and can sense vibrations.

So, the next time you are hell-bent on getting where you want to go, remember how happy a sloth is to travel half a mile in a month. Think you could limit yourself to a single trip like this every 30 days?

When you find yourself speeding up and stressing out, pause, and take a deep breath following the technique opposite.

HOW TO STAY
SAFE

What if you were invisible to predators? Sloths are prey to big birds and big cats, but they move so slow they often go unnoticed by these sharp-clawed, eagle-eyed, razor-beaked birds, and ferocious lightning-fast felines.

When you can only move about 2 inches per second, chances are anything looking for dinner won't even notice you, especially when the stupid monkeys around you are flinging themselves from branch to branch, and tree to tree egging on the hunters on the prowl in search of their next lip-smacking meal.

Whenever you find yourself in danger, seek the safety and protection of a tree (if it works for them it could work for you). Some say they're stupid, but it would be stupid not to mimic one if it saves your life.

Write down what you do when you're scared, and
a few ways you defend yourself.

LET YOUR HAIR DOWN

Sloths have two layers of fur, but they don't go to the hairdresser. How fast does your hair grow? Do you keep it short or do you like it long?

One way to stay invisible is to camouflage yourself with leaf-green algae. Now that you're in sloth school, it's time to grow some on your belly. Of course, if you are terribly concerned with fitting in with societal and cultural norms, simply hop in the shower now and then; you will stay clean and have more friends (and your hair will look nice).

While scientists have found our fungi-farming friends hiding disease-immune antibiotics in their fur, they warn against giving your favorite sloth a tongue bath anytime soon. On the other hand, not worrying about everything all the time may be just the solution. Let your hair down and watch your problems get swept away with the hairdresser's broom.

WHAT COLOR OR STYLE WOULD YOU SPORT IF YOU WERE A SLOTH FOR A DAY?
PULL OUT YOUR MOST COLORFUL PENS AND CREATE THREE DIFFERENT HAIRSTYLES.

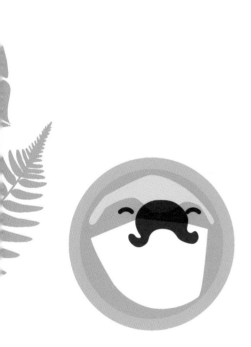

SLOTH IS GOOD

Whoever used sloth as a noun to describe someone going to that place called hell for enjoying a little inactivity had a limited view of the world and their priorities are out of whack. Pious in public and precocious in private was (and is) often the case with these anti-sloth crusaders.

We are often bored with life, but can't seem to embrace The Way of the Sloth. If we could just chill out, everything would be fine. Instead we create all sorts of problems. Chances are you, too, are an introspective, thoughtful type of human and likely know too well all the problems we face.

Just know it's perfectly alright to do nothing every once in a while (especially if there's a chance you could screw things up). Maybe Murphy knew what he was talking about when he said "Anything that can go wrong will." Who says you have to get going or hurry up? Biting your tongue when you have nothing nice to say and waiting to cross the street will always turn out better than doing the opposite.

"IF IT AIN'T BROKE, DON'T FIX IT."

Write down some things that are fine just the way they are.

_____

_____

_____

_____

_____

_____

_____

_____

_____

_____

_____

MORE IS NEVER ENOUGH

When materialism gets out of hand, greed kicks in and it's insatiable. What do sloths own? Nothing, and that's fine with them. Brad Pitt said, "The things we own end up owning us." But we get bored, and then buy even more stuff we won't use.

What is the point? If money can't buy happiness and friends are worth more than gold, why do we believe that consuming more stuff will win us friends and make us happy? Stuff doesn't give us what most of us want more than anything: Love and respect from those we love and respect.

Sloths live a simple life. Simple is sustainable. What is sustainable is successful. Think about the things you own that bring you pleasure or make your life better, and ask yourself what is it about these things that you appreciate.

CIRCLE THE FIVE MOST IMPORTANT THINGS TO YOU IN THIS LIST.

I CAN'T POSSIBLY
LIVE WITHOUT...

1 Toys

2 Pizza

3 Netflix

4 Shoes

5 My dog

6 My cat

7 Art supplies

8 Pen and paper

9 Sunshine

10 Music

11 My stereo

12 Books

13 My bathroom mirror

14 The weekend

15 My best friend

16 My parents

17 Fruit smoothies

18 My bathing suit

19 My sports team

20 Jewelry

21 Water

22 Air

23 Cuddles

24 Love

25 Money

26 The Internet

27 Chocolate

28 Meditation

29 Sleep

30 Electricity

31 Nature

32 Trees

33 My toothbrush

34 Television

35 My bed

36 Shampoo

37 Milkshakes

38 Teddy bear

39 Camera

40 Laptop

41 Swiss army knife

42 Clothes

43 Journal

44 Ice cream

45 Sunscreen

46 Pillows

47 Lip balm

48 Video games

49 French fries

50 Deodorant

PAJAMA PARTY

Why get dressed when you don't have to? Staying in your pajamas and slippers all day instantly qualifies you as an honorary sloth, and you can look forward to these drowsy tree-dwellers welcoming you with open-hooked claws and snuggling in for some love.

Taking it a sloth-step farther (not far at all), make your pajama party a weekly event. Invite some friends over and spend the night creating or crafting while you all munch on hibiscus flower ice cream (which is like chocolate or catnip to sloths).

If anyone ever judges you for your shrewd sense of fashion, don't fall into their trap; it's an illusion. They wish they could wear pajamas and party all day and all night, but can't (or won't, or don't know how) so they judge people who are happy, wild, and free—like you. Try not to let it bother you.

Create a recipe for hibiscus ice cream.

INGREDIENTS

_____

_____

_____

_____

HOW TO

_____

_____

_____

_____

_____

_____

_____

_____

_____

A BOOK IS A DREAM

"A book is a dream you hold in your hand," said Neil Gaiman. You know those stacks of paper filled with words and pictures, bound with glue and wrapped in glossy card stock of varying thickness? For some reason, books still hold symbolic value for people who read, collect, and love them.

If sloths were media-savvy, they would no doubt opt out of screen time in favor of media more suited to their laid-back style. Everyone knows sloths can't read, but that doesn't mean they wouldn't like to be read to by someone with their eyes on the page (not on the pop-up ads geo-targeting them with offers for the zoo they are planning to visit).

Write down your five favorite books on the library cards.

AUTHOR:

TITLE:

DATE:

WHY IT'S THE BEST READ EVER:

AUTHOR:

TITLE:

DATE:

WHY I WILL READ THIS BOOK AGAIN:

AUTHOR:

TITLE:

DATE:

WHY I LOVED THIS BOOK:

AUTHOR:

TITLE:

DATE:

WHY MY BESTIE SHOULD READ THIS BOOK:

AUTHOR:

TITLE:

DATE:

WHY I RECOMMEND THIS BOOK:

DECLUTTER YOUR MIND

Having (or seeking) a solution and answer to every problem that comes up keeps your mind spinning in a vicious cycle and expending more energy than your washing machine. When learning something new, we gather and digest information in various forms and hope it sinks in. What do you think a sloth thinks about all day? How to solve global warming? How to get the bug gut stain out of their fur? They couldn't care less about those things. That's the point; sloths are like little kids—their minds are simple, unmuddled, and uncluttered with the non-essentials of daily life.

What do you think you would gain by emulating the innocent, childlike behavior of a sloth just living from moment to moment?

Rest your head on this page,
close your eyes, and see if
you can think of nothing for

5 SECONDS.

PATIENCE, MY DEAR

Sloths only come down to the ground once a week for a bathroom break, which means they can sure hold it in. On your way from A to B you might also have to stop for a pee break, make a detour, or turn around because you forgot your purse at home. But you don't think twice about the usual delays during the day (unless you are in a rush).

Sloths don't to and fro. There are no comings and goings. Hustle and bustle are a foreign language they will never study. They don't do anything fast. Remember this next time you are stressed out about school work. Instead of huffing and puffing, think: What would a sloth do in this situation?

Dog-ear or bookmark this page so you have something to read the next time you've hurried up just to wait.

"FOR PEACE OF MIND, RESIGN AS GENERAL MANAGER OF THE UNIVERSE."

Larry Eisenburg

TAKE IT EASY

CHILL!

LIMIT
YOUR EXPECTATIONS

To let go of expectations and truly embody your inner sloth, set yourself some simple day-to-day tasks.

If you always keep in mind that what you are expecting may not be expecting you, life will always surprise you. A sloth has few (if any) expectations. And if you only lived for a maximum of 30 years like they do, your expectations would be even less than those in human form. People often overestimate what they can accomplish in one year, though underestimate what they can accomplish in five.

What do you think a sloth expects out of life? The two-ruler-long huggable critters this book is based on are glad to climb 6–8 feet in a minute. Sloths have limited expectations because they have a relatively limited existence. When you get overwhelmed, put yourself in their shoes and see if it makes any difference to your strategy.

PHYSICAL TIME

4

Think beyond the confines of the gym

- [ ] _____
- [ ] _____
- [ ] _____
- [ ] _____
- [ ] _____

FOCUS TIME

1

Spend time focusing intently on one detailed mental exercise

☐ _____
☐ _____
☐ _____
☐ _____
☐ _____

PLAY TIME

2

Allow yourself to be creative and expressive

☐ _____
☐ _____
☐ _____
☐ _____
☐ _____

CONNECTING TIME

3

A moment of deep interpersonal engagement is essential

☐ _____
☐ _____
☐ _____
☐ _____
☐ _____

TIME IN

5

Embody moments where you feel yourself from the inside out

☐ _____
☐ _____
☐ _____
☐ _____
☐ _____

DOWN TIME

6

Give your brain time to integrate the stimuli it has encountered

☐ _____
☐ _____
☐ _____
☐ _____
☐ _____

SLEEP TIME

7

Quality sleep is essential to mental health

☐ _____
☐ _____
☐ _____
☐ _____
☐ _____

SLOTH SELFIES

Selfie tourism (as it is known) promotes animal trafficking and other crimes against our hairy friends. Please admire and appreciate them from afar, but please don't pet, feed, or take photos with them (that's what telephoto lenses are for, or zoom on your smartphone).

Bad people take advantage of our soft spot for snuggly sloths and exploit the species with a built-in smile for the wrong reasons. So if you're thinking of rescuing one, like Green Heritage Fund Suriname founder and director Monique Pool (who rescued 600 sloths, anteaters, armadillos, and porcupines), keep in mind they don't make great pets, and wouldn't adapt well to the big tree in your backyard (as much as you've loved climbing it since you were a kid).

Address a letter to the President of the United States
urging him to save the rainforests and our sloths.

To the President,

NO CARES
IN THE WORLD

In Latin, the word "security" means "without care." In fact, the only beings who enjoy true security are those who have no cares. Apart from risking life and limb while exposing itself out in the open when going to the bathroom, what does a sloth have to worry about?

If you look around, you may notice the most security-minded people are the most unhappy. They are so fearful of change and taking risks, yet freedom from fear is the ability to express yourself and take creative risks. You have to bet big to win big.

What would you do if you had 10 million dollars? What if you had a year to live? What would you do if you knew you couldn't fail? When you know a sloth would take its sweet time engaging in anything inspired by questions like this, you can relax. Life is not a race.

List your biggest fears opposite, watch them fall off the cliff, and feel a weight lift off your shoulders.

PURRRRR

Shhhh. The little sloth is sleeping soundly in the sun-dappled shade of his tree. Too bad you can't curl up next to him, because studies in the UK have shown people sleep better with their pets than with their partners.

The frequency of a cat's purr (25–100 hertz) is well-known in established therapeutic medicine; relaxing with a cat purring on your lap has been shown to reduce your risk of stroke and heart disease by as much as 30 percent. And according to old veterinary lore: "If you put a cat and a bunch of broken bones in the same room, the bones will heal."

Even watching cat videos can bring a smile to your face and calm your nerves. So, if you don't have a sloth lying around, pretend your curled-up cat in a sunny spot on the living room rug is a sloth. If you don't have a cat lying around, get one, because pet owners tend to live longer (they keep you alive because another servant would be too hard to find).

LIST THE WAYS YOUR PET MAKES YOU FEEL BETTER AFTER A BAD DAY.

1 ....
2 ....
3 ....
4 ....
5 ....
6 ....
7 ....
8 ....
9 ....
10 ....
11 ....
12 ....

DO UNTO OTHERS

What does karma mean to you? How about the Golden Rule? Karma means you need to treat others how you would like to be treated, and it is the author's belief that integrity means doing what you say you will do, long after the thrill is gone.

Pretend you believe in reincarnation. What do you think would have had to happen in a past life to show up as a sloth this time around? Do you think they are being rewarded for taking it easy, or are they former busy humans being punished for doing too much?

Like many animals around the world, sloths seem to be peaceful, content creatures. Perhaps they know something we don't: That provoking others is a zero-sum game. Retaliation rarely ends well, so the next time you want to pick a fight with someone try to remember this.

Write the mantra "what goes around comes around" in the mandala opposite to activate your "do unto others" mindset.

REPEAT THE MANTRA UNTIL YOU REACH THE CENTER

YOU BLOOM
WHERE YOU'RE PLANTED

Making the most of what is available (or playing the cards you have been dealt) is a good piece of advice. You are surrounded with all the resources and opportunities you need (you can't take full advantage of everything around you when you're going cheetah-fast and traveling 100 miles per hour).

On the other hand, going snail-slow allows you to stop and smell the roses (and then take another whiff if you feel so inclined). When you take your time, you could decide to pick one and give it to someone else to enjoy.

When a sloth sees a branch loaded with fruit, insects, and leaves that it knows would easily carry its weight, it shimmies out there and doesn't think twice. "Branch. Food. Good. Safe. Go." is likely the anthropomorphic extent of their thought process. What if we applied this sort of systematic simplicity to every situation? Would that slow things down long enough for us to wrap our heads around it?

Take stock of what is around you right this second. List these items on each of the petals below and describe how they make your life better.

HOW TO GET
pERSPECTive

Sloths rarely leave their trees. They aren't globe-trotting, jet-setting digital nomads in search of the next full-moon party; they are quite content to stay home. They know what they have (or don't, but it doesn't matter, because it's all they know). Maybe we have too many options. Maybe we are unable to see the big picture because we don't know what we don't know.

Focus your attention on only one of the smaller parts or aspects of your circumstances, and you will be able to see clues as to what's happening at the scale of the bigger picture. This is how a meticulous, sloth-slow focus on the details can paradoxically provide answers others can't see from 10,000 feet up and going 500 miles an hour.

Why leave your tree? That one is just like yours.

Hold a magnifying glass over this page and see how much detail in the paper and ink you can see.

Focus on the details.

CONSERVE ENERGY

The definition of efficiency is being effective without wasting time, effort, or expense. What would your life be like if you conserved time, effort, and expense? Would it make more time, effort, and money available for the things that were most important to you? Most people have an abundance of all three, yet their priorities are out of whack. Few humans have figured out what makes them happy (and even fewer do what it takes to sustain a consistent state of contentment). Why are so many people frustrated and dissatisfied with their lives?

P.S. Sloths don't have anything to expend, and they seem to get along just fine. Perhaps becoming a lazy loafer, lethargically lumbering our way through existence is the key to a happy and successful life.

Make a habit of working your way through these five simple steps
toward efficiency every day.

FIVE IMPORTANT EVERYDAY STEPS

WEEK COMMENCING	FOCUS ON MOST IMPORTANT TASKS FIRST	BREAK TASKS INTO SMALLER PIECES	DON'T MULTI-TASK	GET BETTER AT SAYING "NO"	TAKE BREAKS, FILL THE TANK, AND RECHARGE
MONDAY					
TUESDAY					
WEDNESDAY					
THURSDAY					
FRIDAY					
SATURDAY					
SUNDAY					

PHOTOCOPY THIS PAGE

THE HAPPINESS OF PURSUIT

What makes a sloth happy? Food, shelter, sunlight, water, and family. What makes you happy? Contrary to popular belief, there are no recipes or secret formulas. When people pursue happiness, it always seems to elude them. On the other hand, some of us learn to enjoy the pursuit, regardless of the outcome.

You have to decide what's important to you, because you may never be fulfilled by the same things other people find satisfying. What's good for the goose ain't good for the sloth. When admiring someone, ask yourself: What does this person believe in? What is important to them? If the answers to these questions align with you and what you want to do, then align yourself with them.

"SUCCESS
is NOT the key to
Happiness.

HAPPINESS
is the KEY to
Success."

Albert Schweitzer

THE PRESENT
MOMENT

What do species with two feet do? They take one step at a time. No matter how fast they move (slow is best), they can only move one step at a time. Of course, the rate at which one steps is closely related to how fast one will get where one hopes to go. But again, why go anywhere? Paraphrasing Eckhart Tolle: if you are anywhere but here, now, you are yearning for something that doesn't exist yet (or anymore) and are thus unhappy about it.

We imagine sloths live blissfully in every moment; eating, sleeping, climbing down the tree once a week for a business meeting, and then back up again. Why are humans blessed (and cursed) with the ability to lament the past while dreaming about the future, when doing so often brings more strife, stress, and suffering than not, and when all we have to do is remember to focus our attention on the present moment?

Focus on the footprints and quote opposite, and
take a moment to enjoy being in the here and now.

"CHANGE THE
WAY YOU LOOK AT
THINGS, AND THE
THINGS YOU LOOK
AT CHANGE."

Wayne Dyer

IT'S ALL GOING SWIMMINGLY

Did you know sloths can swim three times faster than they can walk? That's easy; even humans are essentially weightless in water. Still, if you ever find yourself drowning in the tropical Americas and a sloth swims by, grab on and let them carry you to safety (don't count on them being happy about it; you may get a swat from the X-Men Wolverine-sized claws instead). Sloths can also hold their breath for over 40 minutes, so don't think they're taking a shortcut if they pull you under.

Jokes aside, even though sloths often only leave their trees to go skinny-dipping, and move through the water at triple their land speed, it's still considered dog-paddle slow (their technique actually resembles a dog-paddle/breaststroke combination). As always with sloths, there's no rush and no hurry. So, instead of trying to increase the number of lengths you do in a swim session, take a leaf out of the sloth's book and just enjoy being in the water.

What do you enjoy about being in the water?

WORK LESS AND THINK MORE

Most of us work and study much more than needed. The law of diminishing returns says we eventually get to a point where the benefits we receive don't equal any additional effort.

As you may know, sloths don't have this problem. If you are an extraordinary animal who appreciates this uncommon philosophy, you are a rare ball of brown fur. Definitely do whatever needs to be done, but better yet, learn how to delegate and let others do the heavy lifting for you. When everything is fine and dandy and up to your sloth sub-standards, it's time to slip back into mindfully meditative thought at the serene speed of sloth. Life is way too long to slave away at breakneck speed when a simple shift in thinking (and an ounce or two of creativity) can help you to reach heights the worker bees of the world can't even imagine.

"THE GREATEST GIFT IS THE POWER TO ESTIMATE CORRECTLY THE VALUE OF THINGS."

François, Duc de La Rochefoucauld

List the ways you can work smarter,
not harder. We have started you off.

1 Start your day with a clean workspace. A clear desk equals a clear mind.

2 _____

3 _____

4 _____

5 _____

6 _____

7 _____

8 _____

SLOW
SLOTH CRUMBLE

Sometimes sloths need to switch their diet up and when they do, their go-to dish is apple crumble.

Preheat the oven to a maximum of 325 degrees fahrenheit. Slowly peel, core, and slice four apples. Gradually lift them into a mixing bowl and, without hurrying, add 1/4 cup of sugar, a squeeze of lemon juice, 2 tablespoons of flour, and 1/2 teaspoon of cinnamon. Now, at a leisurely pace, pour into a lightly greased 9 x 13-inch casserole dish and spread into an even layer.

In another bowl, carefully mix together 1 cup of chopped walnuts, 1 cup of all-purpose flour, 1 cup of rolled oats, 1/2 cup of packed brown sugar, 1 teaspoon of ground cinnamon, a pinch of salt, and 1 stick of butter. Using your claws (fingers), gently massage the butter into the mix until you have pea-sized morsels. Tenderly top the apples with this mix and bake until it's golden brown (about 45–60 minutes, but who's watching the clock?). Serve warm or at room temperature and garnish with fresh cecropia (or mint) leaves and vanilla ice cream.

What's your favorite slow bake? Write the recipe opposite.

MY FAVORITE SLOW BAKE

INGREDIENTS

HOW TO

DON'T JUST DO SOMETHING, SIT THERE

Sedentary stillness is soothing to the soul. Why get up and do something when you don't have to? Alternating the fast pace of society with movements like slow cities and slow food may just be the cure to the imbalance pervading our already hectic lives.

For any project or lifestyle to be sustainable, it must abide by earth time. That is, in alliance with the cycles of the natural world in existence for eons. Have you ever been on the water when it was as still as a mirror? How did doing nothing feel?

Productivity is the last thing on a sloth's mind. What is progress? What are we trying to achieve? In reference to the world speeding out of control, Perry Farrell says, "It's lit to pop, and nobody is gonna stop." Meanwhile, our sloth soulmates are content to fall asleep upside down and let every tidbit of troublesome tension pass them by.

Practice the art of doing nothing. Remove all distractions, turn off the TV and your cell phone, and focus on the quote opposite for 5–10 minutes.

"THERE IS MORE
TO LIFE THAN
INCREASING
ITS SPEED."

Mahatma Gandhi

SAVOR THE
SWEET AND SOUR

We can't know one without the other. If we didn't know what salt tasted like, we would be unable to detect, define, and therefore delight in sugar. Just like trying to move a stubborn animal, our tastebuds can't be rushed.

Rushing through a meal is sacrilege. Experts tell us to chew each bite 32 to 40 times. Who does that? Sloths do (and so can you). Though by now you may have realized following in the sanctified footsteps of sloth kind isn't easy. Only the chosen ones will walk The Way of the Sloth, for this journey is a sacred one, not fit for the faint of heart.

Are you worthy? Time will tell, for only the slow and steady are capable of truly savoring the fine flavors of life. It is only by exploring the edges of the extreme that we will find a sense of sedate balance somewhere in the middle (if that's what we're looking for).

Pour some salt on one of the circles below and pour some
sugar on the other. Lick the tip of your finger and taste each one.
Now try mixing them together to concoct the perfect tastebud-tantalizing mix.

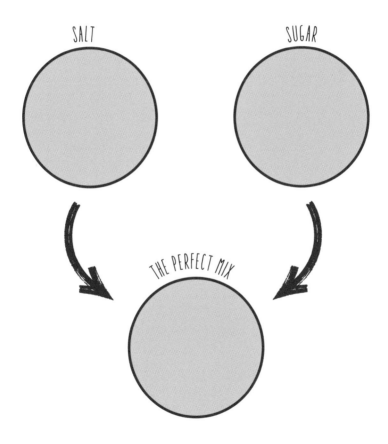

SALT

SUGAR

THE PERFECT MIX

THE MAGIC OF MUSIC

If you went to see a band called The Sloths, what kind of music do you think they would play? Likely serene, ambient electronic music, mild-mannered tunes to soothe savage beasts and encourage every creature in the vicinity to put their feet up for a while, kick back, and enjoy the show.

But what if The Sloths hail from off the grid? Without electricity to plug in their gently electrified sequencers and synthesizers, they would simply resign themselves to producing angelic baroque music and wooing us with romantic four-part harmonies to lull us into sublime submission and eventually into deep slumber. What a peaceful way to fall asleep.

Music and magic are so closely related it would be difficult not to put yourself into a state of sloth by playing some subdued sloth-friendly tunes.

Write down some song titles you listen to
when you want to relax. Here's some
sloth-like songs to start you off.

1   Movin' like molasses

2   Hanging out upside down

3   Going slow is the only way to go

4

5

6

7

8

9

10

11

12

SEDENTARY SOLITUDE

Sloths are solitary souls who rarely connect with each other (this is because they'd rather be curled up into a ball and tucked into a fork in their favorite tree). Can you blame them? If you were introverted, where would you rather be: Going out dancing every night and only getting a few hours of sleep before getting up to go to school the next day, or curled up asleep in a tree for hours on end?

Being by yourself doesn't have to be lonely. In fact, you may find if you're reading a favorite book or working on a favorite project that time just flies by and you don't even notice no one's around. You may be highly productive when you work by yourself. Just because everyone else seems to want to be around people all the time doesn't mean you have to. It's fine to enjoy peace and quiet, and retreat from society if that's what makes you happy.

It's important to be able to enjoy your own company. What are some things you like to do that don't require other people to be around?

- ☐ Read a book
- ☐ Climb a tree
- ☐ Go for a walk
- ☐ Go for an ice cream
- ☐ Write in your journal
- ☐ Think
- ☐ Play music
- ☐ Tidy up
- ☐ Bake a treat
- ☐ Look at old photos
- ☐ Organize your closet
- ☐ Have a nap
- ☐ Write a letter
- ☐ Draw a picture
- ☐ Play Solitaire
- ☐ Ride your bike

- ☐ Make a smoothie
- ☐ Give yourself a pedicure
- ☐ Make a collage
- ☐ Go swimming
- ☐ Master a Rubik's Cube
- ☐ Do yoga
- ☐ Listen to a podcast
- ☐ Do a crossword
- ☐ Start a blog
- ☐ Watch a movie
- ☐ Go stargazing
- ☐ Do a puzzle
- ☐ Meditate
- ☐ Work out
- ☐ Juggle
- ☐ Daydream

THE CALL OF THE
WILD

Sloths live in trees. Some people live in tree houses. Other people build cabins in the wild woods with their bare hands. Still, some folks make pilgrimages across deserts or oceans in search of meaning they feel will only surface while immersed in nature; they are called to travel (by foot, on a horse, by bicycle, or canoe).

Everyone hears the call in some form or another. Some tread the beaten path blazed by others, and choose to never deviate from it. Unfortunately for them, many of these followers end up spending their entire lives doing things they don't enjoy. Yet others know from a young age what lights them up, and they never stop moving and shaking.

The world is yours. Some say it was made for you. What will you do?

Date: ....

Time: ....

Location: ....

My observations: ....

....

....

....

....

....

....

Draw or stick your findings here.

Weather watch

BRILLIANT
BEYOND BELIEF

If you think you're weird (or anyone has ever told you they think you are), consider yourself lucky; it means you're different. It may not seem like it, but being "normal" is boring. You are brilliant beyond belief; you just have to "live the question" and you will find your way. The last thing you want is to be a robot on autopilot, so stop trying to be.

Artists, freaks, weirdos, eccentrics, fruitcakes, and nut-bars unite! You are of the fortunate few. Everyone is creative, but 90 percent of people don't know it and/or do anything about it. Sloths are different. Do you think they care what other sloths think? Do you think they care that some jealous, bitter humans think they're lazy, work-shy slackers?

As long as you don't harm anyone or yourself, you can feel free to express yourself any way you want. Create art, music, clothes, or buildings. Dance, sing, draw, mix, code, sculpt, paint, or sew. You get the picture. You are a rare bird. Fly!

List all the things that make you weirdly wonderful. Write each quirky characteristic on a piece of paper and place in a jar. Open one a day to remind you how special you are.

Wonderful
things
about me

10,000 HOURS

While there are billions of ways to do everything, some sloths
are more skilled than others at finding their favorite eats.
Some sloths are more skilled than others at avoiding predators.
Some sloths are more skilled than others at finding friends.

Sloths have self-esteem and self-confidence. They seem content to
be themselves, intuitively and instinctively living their lives without
doubting themselves or comparing themselves to other sloths.
They are fine with who they are. Are you fine with you?

Because we all do things differently, you have permission to create
a life you love by "making your vocation your vacation." Let sloth
sense guide you when you get impatient. Focus on getting good at what
you love to do, and then get better at it. After about 10,000 hours, you'll
start to see the governing dynamics like Neo did at the end of The Matrix.

How will you get to the end of The Matrix and reach your goal?

START HERE

★ GOAL

GOES DOWN EASY

While two-toed sloths eat everything including small lizards, three-toed sloths are herbivores. When you consider leaves don't have many calories, you can understand why the sages of slow move so slow.

To put it all in perspective, it generally takes us humans about 6–8 hours to digest an entire meal, while it takes a sloth anywhere from a week to a month to digest a single leaf (they must truly savor them).

Eating is such a pleasurable experience for most humans that whether you eat plants or animals, slowing down your digestion probably isn't a good idea. Leave that to the sloths; they've been around longer (which means on some level they are older and wiser).

Drinking water aids digestion and you should aim to drink at least eight glasses a day.

Fill in the glasses opposite to indicate how much water you have drank today.

and for extra bonus points...

THE JOY
OF MISSING OUT

FOMO (the fear of missing out) is defined as "a pervasive apprehension that others might be having rewarding experiences from which one is absent." Furthermore, "This social anxiety is characterized by a desire to stay continually connected with what others are doing."

Exhausting! And it's the last thing any self-respecting sloth would dwell on for more than a blink of their beady little eyes. As a sloth sympathizer, your natural inclination would be not to worry your fuzzy little head about such trifling trivialities, correct?

When you see things how they are (not how you wish them to be) you will find freedom where others sadly suffer. But they have to figure it out on their own, remember? How do you combat such Saturday night terrors when they threaten your tranquil serenity?

What do you enjoy about staying in?

_____

_____

_____

_____

_____

_____

_____

_____

_____

_____

_____

_____

_____

_____

SLOTH SHANGRI-LA

The life span of a sloth is 30 years. How old are you? What would you do differently if you only lived as long as the world's most blissfully inactive mammal? Why do anything except express your unique brand of love and kindness in the service of not only your own soul, but in the service of others so they may be saved from the horrors of burnout?

As we age, all sloths among us (if they are of the reflective, mindful sort) become more altruistic. When someone has been around the block and seen a thing or two, as long as they can avoid becoming weary and jaded, the hard-won wisdom they have earned ripens them like fine wine or sharp cheese, or anything else that gets better with age.

Sloths take time in their stride. They don't rush or rally or race through life. They are content with little and their lives are simple. They have evolved over eons to require less, yet we are only now catching on. Luckily, the longer you live, the greater your chance of arriving at Sloth Shangri-la.

SHINRIN-YOKU

Trees and plants provide shelter and protection for birds, insects, and animals.

Japan is the birthplace of what is known as the art of forest bathing, though sloths were likely hip to the physical, emotional, and spiritual benefits long before the Japanese (or anyone else) coined the phrase.

A gentle, anyone-can-do-it approach to holistic healing, the philosophy and practice of shinrin-yoku (intentionally spending time in the forest) clearly has its benefits (which clearly outweigh the drawbacks). What could be better than hanging out with trees and breathing fresh forest air every day of your life?

Preventive natural medicine is simple. Fortunately, when you venture on or off the beaten path, planning to soak up the peace and quiet of the countryside or a city park on your way home from school, the natural world comes alive to tantalize your five senses and fold you into sloth culture.

Immerse yourself in the forest and reap the benefits of nature's gift to man (and sloths).

Plants cure diseases.

KEEP IT SIMPLE SLOTH

The acronym KISS is famous. First known as "Keep It Simple Stupid," this author would frequently rework it as "Keep It Simple Sweetheart." Thanks to this book, this sugarcoated criticism has farther evolved: To truly Keep It Simple Sloth, one must abide by a code of conduct, and therefore ascribe to the tenets of simplicity, sustainability, and (the spirituality of) slowing down.

Move modestly with humility. Listen to someone tell a story. Allow people to move at their chosen clip. Let others make their own decisions. Learn how to get results in the least amount of time, with the least amount of effort. Celebrate your simple successes.

Remind yourself every day to take it slow. Revel in this awareness that is likely counterintuitive to what you've been taught. There is beauty in slow and soft, light and tender. Touch everyone and everything with kindness, compassion, and patience, and you will transform your life.

How do you live by the KISS code? Write each aspect you practice in the lips opposite.

"THINGS THAT MATTER
MOST MUST NEVER BE AT
THE MERCY OF THINGS
THAT MATTER LEAST."

Johann Wolfgang von Goethe

SLOTH-IAL MEDIA

With their uniquely furry form of self-confidence, it doesn't appear sloths worry too much about keeping up with their neighbors going by the last name Jones. Social media is a blessing and a curse. On one hand, it provides a window into what family and friends are up to (do you notice how many portray a model life?). Comparing ourselves to our peers when we feel far from perfect can drive even the slowest of the slow into an anxiety attack trying to attain unparalleled utopia.

On the other hand, these creatively coded suites of software not only connect us, but also allow us to celebrate the ups and downs of the people we care about most.

If you ever find yourself judging your circumstances based on the false fear that you don't measure up to the beautiful people posting flawlessly fictitious "perfect" photos, it's okay to log off and remember why you registered for an account in the first place: To share your love of sloths with the world!

Noticing how social media makes you feel can help you discover how to use it more mindfully. As you become more aware of the emotions you are inviting into your day when you visit these sites, you'll be able to make better decisions about how often to visit them. Try this social media mindfulness practice to explore what your favorite sites are communicating to your subconscious.

1 Find a comfortable, alert, and ready posture. Shrug your shoulders, take a few breaths, and bring awareness to your physical and emotional state.

2 Before you open your favorite social media site, consider your intentions and expectations. As you focus on the icon, notice what experiences you have in your mind and body.

3 Why are you about to check this site? What are you hoping to see or not see? How are you going to respond to different kinds of updates you encounter? Are you interested in connecting or disconnecting?

4 Close your eyes and focus on your emotional state for three breaths before you begin to engage. Opening your eyes, look at the first status update or photo, then sit back and close your eyes again.

5 Notice your response and emotion. Is it excitement? Boredom? Jealousy? Regret? Fear? How do you experience this emotion in the mind and body? What's the urge—to read on, to click a response, to share yourself, or something else?

6 Wait a breath or two for the sensations and emotions to fade, then focus on your breath, body, and surrounding sounds.

FIESTA VS. SIESTA

Sloths tend to party less than the average monkey or baboon so it's a foregone conclusion: You are likely long-lost kith and kin of sloth kind, for no slug-slow mammal in their right mind would ever party like it's 1999.

Studies show that grabbing some afternoon shut-eye nuzzled in the shady fronds of your cecropia tree can boost your memory power faster than upgrading the RAM in your computer, though sleep experts suggest limiting your daily doze to 1,800 seconds (20 minutes) or you'll end up sleeping so soundly you won't want to wake up and get back to work.

Need to recharge? Don't lean on sugary drinks. Take a leaf out of the sloth's book and get some shut eye. A power nap will boost your memory, cognitive skills, creativity, and energy levels.

The 20-minute power nap is good for alertness and motor-learning skills like typing and playing the piano.

30-60
MINUTES

20
MINUTES

Slow-wave sleep (30–60 minutes of shut-eye) is good for decision-making skills, such as memorizing vocabulary or recalling directions.

Getting rapid eye movement (REM) sleep of 60–90 minutes plays a key role in making new connections in the brain and solving creative problems.

60-90
MINUTES

PRIORITIES

As the story goes, there was once a laid-back fisherman who lived in
a tropical country. Every day he would get up and go fishing for a few
hours, catch enough fish for supper, then play with his children,
and go out with his friends to have fun and play music.

One day a high-powered CEO from a more developed country was lolling
around the dock when the two of them began talking. The businessman saw
an opportunity, and couldn't contain himself. "Why don't you work 12 hours
a day, buy more boats, catch more fish, and export it to other
countries?" he asked. The fisherman responded,
"Why would I do that?"

The executive didn't even blink. "With more boats and
more fishermen, you could build an empire, sell it, and
retire. Then you could move down to a tropical country, catch
a few fish every morning, spend time with your family, and have
fun and play music all night with your friends."

We have to learn how to want what we already have in our lives.
Wanting what we have doesn't mean everything is "perfect," or
that we can't desire for things to change or evolve in a way we deem
positive. It simply means we choose to accept what we have in our
life, right now, with a sense of gratitude and surrender.

In each fish, write what you are grateful for in your life.

UNCONDITIONAL
LOVE

Loving all the other animals in the kingdom you care about is easy. But when it comes to those species who tend to always rub your fur the wrong way, it's difficult to muster the patience, kindness, and respect they deserve (regardless of how fast they're moving or how aggressively they act).

It costs nothing to be kind. What if we were kind and compassionate to everyone we met, regardless of who they were, what they eat, what they wear, what they do every day, or how fast or slow they go?

Don't you want the same freedom to be yourself without being judged?

This visualization exercise can help you to experience love on an energetic level.

1

Put your hands over your heart and imagine your favorite color.

2

Close your eyes and visualize your body filling up with this vibrant color.

3

Picture this color radiating out of you in all directions.

4

Feel the warm glow making you and everyone around you happy.

5

Smile like a sloth, knowing you are a fountain of unconditional love.

FORGIVENESS

Sloths hold no resentment toward others (maybe due to the fact they are perpetually in the present moment). If you lived like there was no future nor past, you could do this too, but unfortunately, we hold onto hurt long after the perpetrator has forgotten all about the event (and sometimes us).

Focus on the quote opposite and think of those you need to forgive. Let go of resentment and regret.

"By not forgiving someone,
you block your own chance
to grow up and become a
fully functioning adult.
You continue to see yourself
as a victim. Even worse,
you keep your negative
feelings of inferiority
and anger alive."

Brian Tracy

SLOW
IS THE NEW
FAST

Imagine driving a sports car in a high gear all day. You wouldn't get very far. When you shift into a lower gear, you not only reduce fuel consumption, but your engine also doesn't have to work as hard. When you are relaxed and calm, your creative spirit soars and your mind becomes like a still pond on a windless day.

Ask any philosopher, inventor, or creative genius and they will all agree: The best ideas come when you're in a calm state of mind. Russian chemist Dmitri Mendeleev was fast (asleep) one day, dawdling drowsily in dreamland. When he woke up, he picked up a pencil and drew the periodic table of elements. What will you create when your inner engine is purring in (s)low gear?

Write (in each element) one word to remind yourself of why staying in the slow lane is the fastest way to get where you want to go.

THE PAGES
INSIDE
THE BOOK

Do you have a crystal ball? Can you see what's coming around the bend? Sloths can't see the future, but they are able to rotate their heads almost 270 degrees. That's like having eyes in the back of their heads. What a unique perspective that must be!

There exists a saying that goes: "When you assume, you make an ass out of you and me." Have you ever put your foot in your mouth but didn't have any ketchup to go with it? Have you ever jumped to conclusions before you knew what was really happening? How did that turn out?

When you meet someone new, do you fondly welcome them into your fold of friends, intuiting their brilliant beauty between the covers of their book, or do you instantly brush them off with brazen boldness? What makes you do this?

Apart from outer appearance, what do you find beautiful in the world? Get some magazines, scissors, and glue and make a collage. As you browse, clip, and glue, ask yourself if each image you choose actually represents what lies beneath the surface.

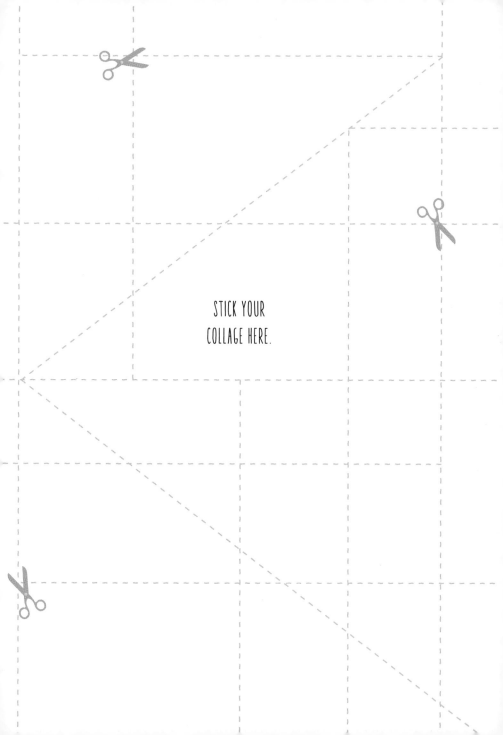

STICK YOUR
COLLAGE HERE.

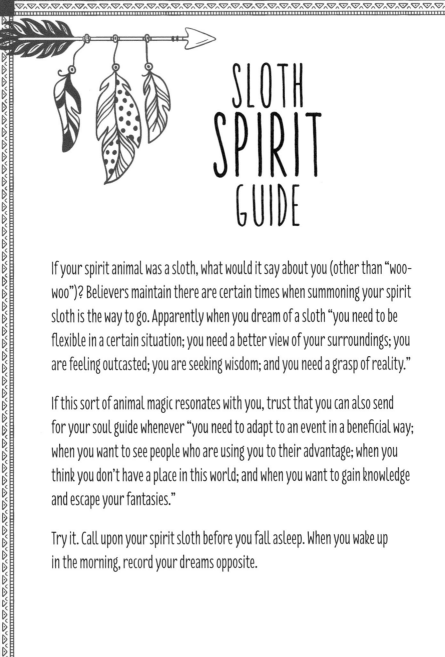

SLOTH SPIRIT GUIDE

If your spirit animal was a sloth, what would it say about you (other than "woo-woo")? Believers maintain there are certain times when summoning your spirit sloth is the way to go. Apparently when you dream of a sloth "you need to be flexible in a certain situation; you need a better view of your surroundings; you are feeling outcasted; you are seeking wisdom; and you need a grasp of reality."

If this sort of animal magic resonates with you, trust that you can also send for your soul guide whenever "you need to adapt to an event in a beneficial way; when you want to see people who are using you to their advantage; when you think you don't have a place in this world; and when you want to gain knowledge and escape your fantasies."

Try it. Call upon your spirit sloth before you fall asleep. When you wake up in the morning, record your dreams opposite.

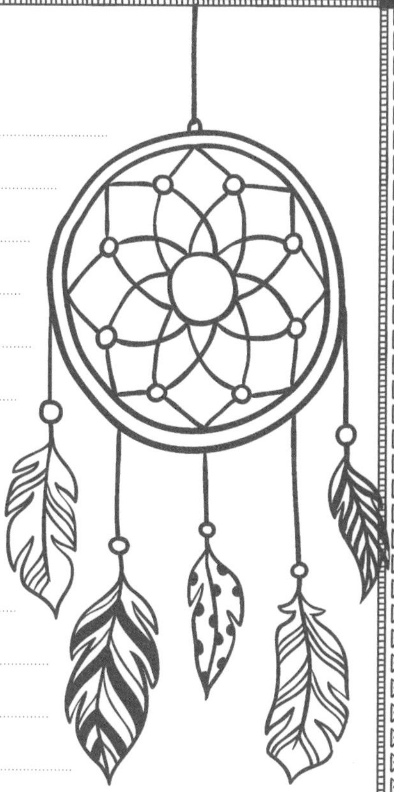

YOUR BODY IN
BALANCE

The secret to a long and slothful life is balance. Yin and yang, light and dark, sweet and sour. You get the picture. The Chinese believe one indication of your overall health is how your chi (life force) is flowing along the energetic meridians of your body.

If like most sloths, you are happy to only exert yourself if and when necessary, the relaxed, gentle movements of chi gong or tai chi may be just the thing you need to bring your life back into balance (or maintain it if you're already steady).

Standing still, pull in your catch in your imaginary fishing net while slowly breathing in, then throw it back into the imaginary sea as you exhale. Or while composedly posing like a crouching tiger, tranquilly burst into action and pretend to pounce on your mythological prey. These calm, back-and-forth meditative gestures cultivate, circulate, and harmonize your chi and can improve your balance, posture, coordination, flexibility, and endurance.

Focus on the symbol opposite and practice your own daily meditative movements to find your inner sloth.

CITTASLOW

Inspired by the slow food movement, Cittaslow is an organization whose goals include "improving the quality of life in towns by slowing down its overall pace."

If you live in a town of less than 50,000 sloths and things already seem to be moving at a snail's pace, and if you can meet at least 50 percent of the eligibility requirements, apply to join the worldwide movement whose aims include: Improving quality of life in cities; resisting the homogenization of towns around the globe; protecting the environment; promoting cultural diversity and the uniqueness of individual cities; and providing inspiration for a healthier lifestyle.

Once you are finished procrastinating a little longer and if this sounds like something you could eventually get around to getting behind, see if the powers-that-be in your small town see the benefits of cultural enrichment via stepping on the brakes.

Make a list of 10 benefits your city or town would enjoy by adopting a slower pace of life.

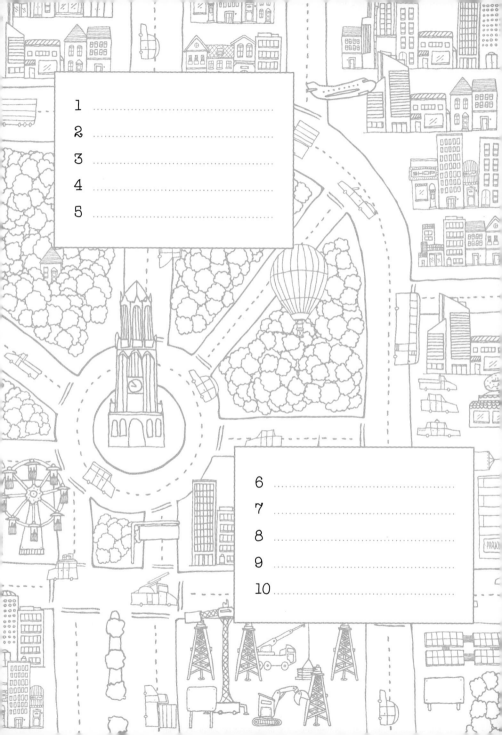

1 ....
2 ....
3 ....
4 ....
5 ....

6 ....
7 ....
8 ....
9 ....
10 ....

EVERYTHING IN MODERATION

Sloths are models of moderation and saints of self-restraint. These seemingly sweet-tempered memes who nuzzle their way into our lives and tug on our heartstrings have much to teach us. Why not chew on a leaf from the book of sloth (not this one) and tether and temper your enthusiasm when celebrating the cutest and cuddliest in the animal realm?

Philosophers regularly remind us to approach everything in moderation, even moderation. Yes, you are being encouraged to imitate and emulate the positive aspects of slothful slothfulness so you may cultivate a more conscious existence, and therefore enjoy your life a whole lot more. This is the reason you are reading this book.

In your lifelong quest for your personal set-point of whatever qualities and experiences you seek, the farther you go in one direction, the more inevitable it is you will then swing equally as far in the opposite direction. Keep in mind that whatever you want may perpetually slip through your fingers, so keep your smiley head on your shoulders.

Write down seven things that excite you most about your life. Contemplate each one, then describe how taming your enthusiasm may make it even better.

1

2

3

4

5

6

7

POST-ENLIGHTENMENT

As the ancient zen proverb "Before enlightenment, chop wood, carry water. After enlightenment, chop wood, carry water" reminds us, the mundane aspects of life such as schoolwork, caring for pets, and cleaning your room will always need doing.

Just because you have "seen the light" in a lucid dream, or had a religious experience cradled in the treetops, doesn't mean you get to pack your bags and hop on the next flight to another dimension (even though it beckons brightly).

Lo, once we have transcended the illusion of separateness and become aware that our claws, the tree they're wrapped around, the leaves we like to eat, and our small lethargic bodies are all connected on a subatomic level, we have a greater responsibility to be even more present and patient with the chores, duties, and people in our lives.

Take pleasure in the small things in life. Remember the joy of receiving a new book, opening it without breaking the spine, and inhaling that new book smell? Do it. Do it now!

INHALE HERE

MORE FREE TIME

Not to alarm you, but one day robot sloths will be doing the grunt work. They won't need coffee breaks or days off. They will make fewer mistakes (if any) and do everything nanosecond fast (the opposite of you). Be prepared...

STEP 1

Learn how to relax so you won't be so offended when it happens.

STEP 2

Start thinking about the kinds of things robot sloths won't be able to do.

STEP 3

Now that you're off the hard work hook, you have more free time to laze around or do more of the things you enjoy with the people you love.

The slower you go, the more time you have. There's no reason to rush around like a headless chicken waiting for the sky to crumble like a crispy cookie. Put away your watch and you will be wealthier than many billionaires who don't enjoy the luxury of free time. Start yesterday.

WHAT WOULD YOUR TYPICAL DAY LOOK LIKE IF YOU HAD MORE TIME TO DO WHAT YOU LOVE?

PERFECTION

What is perfect in your life? Unless the answer is nothing, go find your inner lion, or tiger, or bear. Sloths don't care about being perfect. They don't care about having the best body, grades, toys, friends, clothes, or trophies. At best, a stimulating social life and millions of material possessions only complicate life. Striving to be perfect in every way distorts the perception of reality because nothing is ever perfect. Worse, it makes less productive/ successful animals around you jealous.

Striving to be the bee's knees or cat's pajamas ain't what it's cracked up to be. Sloths don't care what their hair looks like. They don't care what kind of backpack or shoes they wear, nor do they give a weekly bowel movement about posting picture-perfect photos of their latest victories on social media. Forget having the last word; your inner sloth will find you when you are blind to your imperfect, dreadlocked, wiry, cow-licked fur while grooming yourself before bed.

Follow these five steps to soothe your desire to be perfect. Instead, find perfection in imperfection.

1
Tackle your fear of failure.

2
Grow from mistakes.

3
Appreciate compliments and
celebrate your accomplishments.

4
Accept who you are.

5
Repeat.

FASHION

What would you wear if you were going to a party tonight?
Do you have a favorite outfit? How does it make you feel?
What does it say about you? Who would you be without it?

Whether you buy your own clothes (or are talented and inclined
to make your own) the designs, cuts, and colors you choose say
a lot about you (or the people you identify with most). Who
influences what you wear? Do you ever see yourself as a pioneering
trendsetter? Are you drawn to expensive, in-vogue, custom haute
couture, or do you find yourself as happy as a sloth browsing
through last year's clearance rack at the thrift store?

In the end, if you don't like doing laundry (and wish you could just
wear the same thing every day like sloths do) enroll in private
school. That is, of course, unless you pride yourself in your keen
fashion sense and the world needs to know you got it going on.

Sketch your favorite outfit on the sloth opposite.

DRESS ME UP!

MONEY IN THE ANIMAL KINGDOM

Think of your allowance like water. Is your water bottle filled to the brim every week as planned, or is it only half-full because you didn't do your chores? Regardless of how much you receive, be like a beaver and build a dam so it all doesn't flow through your fingers for another sloth downstream to enjoy. Savvy savers and cautious consumers, sloths trust in time and manage their money carefully. They also take notes from their squirrel sidekicks who store their loot in their tree trunk safes for safekeeping.

Think of your money as transportation; it gets you where you want to go at the speed you are inclined (a sloth's RPMs rarely reach the redline, and their odometer rarely exceeds 25 miles per hour). Remember: the humble tortoise won the race while the arrogant hare was fast asleep, assured of victory.

Every dollar you save you get to keep. Tape a $1 bill here to remind yourself that saving a dollar is the same as earning it.

STICK HERE

SLOWTH TRAVEL

Two feet. Two wheels. Two hands (if you are one of those people who can walk on your hands). That's all it takes to get somewhere. Two oars. Two sails. Two pedals. Heck, if you really want to go for a ride, become an astral traveler and seek out the inexplicable at the furthest reaches of space and then come back and tell the rest of us about it.

Consider how sloths get from A to B. They don't rush. They move like molasses. If they drove, they would drive slowly. Ever consider walking or riding a bike instead of being driven? If the journey is the destination (meaning the destination and journey are one—the place you find yourself, wherever that may be), the more self-sufficiently you get there under your own steam and the more sensitive your finger is to the pulse of the experimental adventure called life.

DESCRIBE YOUR ULTIMATE ADVENTURE.

_____

_____

_____

_____

_____

_____

_____

_____

_____

_____

_____

_____

_____

MY ADVENTURE
STARTS HERE

THE SCIENCE OF ART

You might say if there was a science to art, it would be called science, not art. But wait. When you are firing a clay pot, that kiln has got to be hot (1,900 degrees Fahrenheit to be exact). When mixing paint, every painter has their own process and secret formula. And we can thank the innate mathematical sensibilities of songwriters and composers for why we like one piece of music more than another.

How does this relate to finding your inner sloth? Sloths are a form of art. We marvel in and at their unapologetic display of effortless effortlessness, enchanted by their apparent carelessness, and absolutely dumbstruck by one of nature's most simple expressions of life on four legs.

We are captivated by sloths in the same way we stand awestruck in front of a centuries-old masterpiece in an art gallery on the other side of the world. Nature is both a brilliant artist and gifted scientist.

What is art? What is science? If you see more art in your life, color the beaker blue. If you see more evidence of science, color the beaker red. If it's a mix, color it to the degree you believe each is present in your life.

ART VS.
SCIENCE IN
YOUR LIFE

SLOW LEARNERS

If you have any desire to grow and change and explore new things, you will be faced with the challenge of adapting to your environment. There is no limit to what you can learn (and based on the outlook from the biotech industry, we ain't seen nothing yet).

You may live a very long time and have the opportunity to learn things humans currently imagine near-impossible. Regardless of how much you want to absorb and accomplish, developing patience and determination will serve you your entire life.

If you are a slow learner or late bloomer, you can be confident that sloths everywhere share your protracted ability to outwit the bright but short-lived one-hit wonders by employing a steady sense of delayed timing.

When you turn the page, see if you can do it so slowly that it takes you a minute to do it.

S-L-O-W-L-Y TURN THE PAGE

SLOW VS. STUPID

Some people use the word "slow" as a nice way of saying "stupid," like the joke "Sloths are so stupid they mistake their own arm for a branch." If you have ever been called stupid (or slow), be rubber, because the person who thinks they are judging you is glue; they can't help it, they are unconsciously scared they don't measure up to society's expectations.

If they weren't keenly aware of their own lack of abilities on an unconscious level, you wouldn't even show up on their radar. Sadly, they think the same of anyone who isn't like them. Just remember that no one knows you like you do.

How many synonyms can you come up with for the word slow?
(Answers in the back of the book.)

SLOW BREAD

Combine the following in a mixing bowl: 4 cups of all-purpose flour, a tablespoon of salt, a pinch of instant yeast, and 2.5 cups of water. Cover with plastic wrap for 18 hours and let the tick-tock of time on the clock do the work for you.

Eighteen hours later, put a Dutch oven or large casserole dish with a lid in the oven and preheat to 400 degrees Fahrenheit. Sprinkle the counter with flour, and with floured fingers pull the dough out of the bowl and shape into a ball, letting it rest on the counter until the oven reaches the desired temperature. Remove the Dutch oven from the oven and keep the oven mitt on the lid to remind you that it's hot. Carefully drop the dough into the Dutch oven, cover, and bake for 30 minutes. Remove the lid and bake for another 15–30 minutes until the top is the color you like. Cool on an oven rack before slicing and save the crispy, caramel-colored crumbs.

Write your favorite slow cooker recipe opposite.

MY FAVORITE RECIPE

INGREDIENTS

HOW TO

1

2

3

4

5

VOLUNTARY SIMPLICITY

Like many creatures who don't do much all day, sloths live very simple lives. One reason humans are stressed out all the time is because they derive great pleasure in over-thinking everything and adding convoluted complexity wherever possible.

Intentionally surrendering a complicated existence in favor of a simple one doesn't mean quitting school, living in a cardboard box, flushing your toothbrush, and going dumpster-diving for dinner.

It means choosing to minimize unnecessary stress, aggravation, and anxiety by spending less and saving more; opting to walk or bike instead of getting into a car; eating whole foods versus packaged and processed foods; consuming fewer resources that when wasted contribute to increased pollution; and not upgrading just because the new model can do Z and yours only does the entire alphabet up to Y.

List five ways you can change your life by consuming less or by simplifying things.

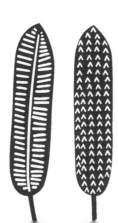

ZYMOLOGY

Since the beginning of recorded history, humans have been engaged in the science of fermentation; turning grape juice into wine, honey into mead, and grain into bread. You can turn cucumbers into dill pickles, milk into tangy yogurt, tea into fizzy kombucha, and cabbage into sour sauerkraut, all by letting the slow passing of time and the microscopic world of microorganisms do all the work for you.

The science: When you are fermenting, you are converting the sugars and carbohydrates into alcohol or other organic acids along with carbon dioxide, giving you a variety and diversity of flavors, aromas, and textures to rice, grains, beans, fruit, fish, vegetables, dairy, and meat products. If you can eat it, you can slowly ferment it, enriching your food with essential amino acids and vitamins. What will you brew up in the kitchen today?

List the fermented foods you have tried.

"BE LIKE A POSTAGE STAMP. STICK TO ONE THING UNTIL YOU GET THERE."

Josh Billings

SINGLE-TASKING

Research suggests multi-tasking can reduce how productive you are by 40 percent which proves we are not designed to function at our best when we are juggling tasks, duties, and responsibilities like we are circus performers.

The joke is that multi-tasking is an opportunity to screw up more than one thing at a time. It's not only less efficient (switching gears back and forth can short-circuit our transmissions), but it also makes life more complicated. When seeking slothful serenity, who needs more stress and anxiety? Don't you want to be happier, feel healthier, and make better decisions? By focusing on a single thing at a time, you will make fewer mistakes. Don't let speedy society stifle your creative cognitive abilities by suggesting (or forcing) you to do too many things at once. Enter the lazy river orbit of sloth-dom, because by chasing two rabbits you won't catch either. You're welcome.

SLOTH POWER!

The difference between the slow and steady power of the sloth and the forces that persuade the slow and steady to get up and go, are clear. Sloth power is yielding, flowing, relaxed, loose, accepting, and inclusive, whereas the well-meaning motivating forces of progress suggest (if not demand) we conquer these "soft" energies with harder, forceful, aggressive, and assertive action-oriented energies. Sloth power is sustainable; it is a metaphor for how things happen on their own timeline. You can't force grass to grow or a flower to bloom. You can't force yourself to like someone, and you can't make your friend, or mom, or dad do something they don't want to do. Why does everyone keep trying to change things that can only change when nature is good and ready?

Trust the timing of your life. You don't need to have everything sorted by the age of 30. List all of the things that you have to look forward to and enjoy fulfilling them in your own time.

1 _____

2 _____

3 _____

4 _____

5 _____

6 _____

7 _____

8 _____

9 _____

10 _____

11 _____

12 _____

13 _____

14 _____

15 _____

CONTINUE YOUR LIST ON A SEPARATE SHEET
OF PAPER AND ATTACH TO THIS PAGE.

GET OFF THE GRID

Have you ever considered going on a digital diet? That means consuming fewer pixels than you need to function (in other words, doing things in the real world that don't involve WiFi). If you are attracted to living like a sloth, you are aware that humans still enjoy eye contact, shaking hands, talking face-to-face, hugging, and listening with their ears (instead of with their earbuds). Hopefully you haven't gone too far down the rabbit hole. Hopefully many of the ideas and activities in this book are gentle, approachable, and enjoyable (like a sloth). If you agree, you are not as far gone as perhaps some of your peers. And if this is the case, you probably don't need to be reminded to ignore the inescapable jeers and judgment that may be aimed in your direction if you choose to go on a digital diet every now and then.

Record how long you spend on your phone, laptop, tablet, and watching TV under the apps opposite.

ON MY CELLPHONE
DATE......................
TIME SPENT..............

PLAYING GAMES
DATE......................
TIME SPENT..............

WATCHING TV
DATE......................
TIME SPENT..............

TABLET
DATE......................
TIME SPENT..............

EVERYTHING IS TEMPORARY

Nothing is permanent. Not you, not the earth, not the sun, not your problems. Knowing this, any sloth with an ounce of dignified self-confidence will relax even more, settling into another slumber even deeper than the mid-morning nap before lunch. Sloths are all about the fleeting short-term. As you may have gleaned by now, they live completely in the present. And when anyone lives in the present moment, neither the future nor the past matter. They know everything is constantly in flux, so why fight it? What has lasted in your life? What is the same as it used to be? Change is the only constant you can rely on, so why fret when things don't seem to be going your way? For this reason, all problems are interim frustrations. Brighter days are on the horizon, and the sun is always shining; it's just behind the clouds. Remember: "This too shall pass."

CHANGE?

What does change look like to you?

List 10 things that you believe are changing for the better.

1

2

3

4

5

6

7

8

9

10

JUST SAY

NO!

"No," the third most important word in the human language (the first is your name, the second is yes), shouldn't be limited in its use. This magic word is a suitable response to most offers and questions you receive in the course of your day (or your life), especially if you want to stay enrolled in the School of Sloth. How often do you say yes when you mean the polar opposite? You can disagree. You can diverge and clash if you so feel like it. No self-respecting sloth says yes to any request that will move them farther out of their comfort zone than is comfortable. Of course, expanding your horizons by stealing a glance at the tree on the corner now and then (even though the leaves aren't greener) is acceptable, because it will only reconfirm your commitment to living your life as you see fit, thank you very much.

Under what circumstances is NO an acceptable answer? (Hint: You can say it as often as you want).

THINK OF EVERY POSSIBLE CIRCUMSTANCE
YOU CAN AND WRITE IT DOWN HERE.

YOU HAVE A
CHOICE

Not making a choice is a choice you can feel satisfactory about. Taking a moderate stance on any issue is just what a sloth would do. How are they supposed to decide anything? Regardless of whether sloths learn from their mistakes, we can contemplate and ponder over and over until we feel fine about our decisions. In fact, once we have made a big decision, we tend to justify it in any way we can. That's how sloths (and we) sleep at night. Fearing what may or may not happen often turns out to be much worse than actually making a decision, learning from it, and moving on, so what are you afraid of?

You always have options. The question is: How creative are your solutions? Describe a recent situation when you made a decision you were proud of.

COMING OF AGE

Physical fitness. Vitamins. Hair in your ears (or covering your entire body). Sloths can live up to 30 years (which is how long humans used to live prior to the advent of antibiotics and an understanding of the importance of personal hygiene). Old humans around you are good models for finding your inner sloth. More often than not they tend to move slow, think slow, and eat slow. What better example of the personified sloth lifestyle than observing elderly folks? P.S. They're everywhere.

Thing is, they have been around the block a few more times than you; they've seen things you may never see; they know things it will take you a lifetime to know (that's if you learn it at all). Respect for seniority is a sign of maturity. Sloths know those big old maple trees are perfect for tapping. You may not fill your pitcher with enough sap to fill your pot, but the syrup you make from the wisdom they spout will be rich and full of flavor.

When was the last time you sought advice from the elderly? What did they say? Write down what you learned (or think you can learn if you have yet to interview a gray-haired sage of the ages).

GREAT ADVICE!

FOLLOW YOUR
INTUITION

Ever notice that no matter how hard you will something, things turn out better than you could have planned? When was the last time you left 10 seconds earlier or later than you would ordinarily have, only to run into a friend that wouldn't have been there had either of you been a bit early or running late? Once you start paying attention, you will notice it all the time. The point is to trust it—certain your intuition is running on auto-pilot to ensure you're clawing your way up the right tree at the right time. You have control over your thoughts, feelings, and actions, or do you?

How often have you ignored the little voice inside only to say, "I should have listened to my intuition. I knew that was going to happen. Next time I'll listen." Be patient with yourself. Learning to rely on your sixth sloth sense in the future will lead you in the right direction.

IMAGINE YOU HAD A DIRECT LINE TO YOUR INTUITION—
NO DROPPED CALLS—WHAT WOULD IT SAY?

INFINITY

Out beyond the farthest reaches of time and
space lie extra-terrestrial sloth-like creatures
slow on the uptake, going about their business in their
trademark slacker style. What do you imagine life is like
out past the borders and bounds of what we know (or assume)
exists? If there is life on other planets, thriving in other
galaxies, and swimming in far-off solar systems, how fast
do you think it's all moving? Considering the possibility that limits
don't exist (and that sloth-like critters may very well be wandering
or floating around in zero gravity at the edges of space), you are
granted permission to find your stride and take the steps you
feel ready and able to take in your own time. The rate
and velocity at which you vibrate in the limitlessness
of life is up to you.

Make a list of what you believe is possible,
and a list of what you think is impossible.
What's the difference?

POSSIBLE
STUFF

IMPOSSIBLE
STUFF

PLAY

What do you like to do in your free time? What do you imagine and pretend is real? What toys or tools do you play with when you're not at school? Sloths play just like you do. Watch them learn to climb, meandering their way through a jungle gym; they are adorable, looking at you with an upside-down frown. It's okay. Go and see for yourself. This book can wait. Playfulness is the secret to pure happiness, and don't let a supersonic Sporty Spice type who has bitten off more than she can chew tell you any different (chances are the last time this over-achiever played just to play was last day of kindergarten). Like many of the cures presented to you in this book to relieve the threatening ills of society, making play a (big) part of your day will also lower your blood pressure, reduce your risk of (d)anger, and allow your body, mind, and spirit to work together in harmony.

When your inner child comes out, what games do you play (with them)? List some in the boxes opposite.

ROLL OUT THE MAT

If you practice yoga, you may already notice the innumerable benefits. But try to tell a newbie what it's all about and your passionate enthusiasm for the Eastern philosophy and practice of twisting yourself into a pretzel can fall on skeptical ears. Improved flexibility may be the most obvious benefit of a yoga practice, but aches and pains regularly disappear, and you can realign your spine if it's been a little wonky and out of whack from all the snoozing and hanging around doing nothing all day. Get to the point where you can do a handstand and you will be able to climb any tree and do anything thanks to the increased blood flow and decreased blood pressure, corrected posture, and lowered resting heart rate. And with less cortisol fueling your animal instincts, you will make better sloth decisions based on possibility versus fear of lack.

WHAT YOGA POSES ARE YOU GOING TO ATTEMPT TODAY?

THE TAO OF SLOTH

What is more important than finding inner peace? Knowing what you're about and what's important to you is how you find your own zen. Sloths are the poster animals for this pinnacle of experience with the cool name from the Eastern hemisphere. Watch the sunrise or sunset from your treetop. If you have a fireplace, use it. Throw your alarm clock away and sleep until you wake up naturally. Get a massage. Make snow angels. Revisit the religion you grew up with. Drink exotic tea. Buy yourself flowers. There are billions of ways to find your inner sloth.

"IT IS VAIN TO SAY HUMAN BEINGS OUGHT TO BE SATISFIED WITH TRANQUILITY. THEY MUST HAVE ACTION, AND WILL MAKE IT IF THEY CANNOT FIND IT."

Charlotte Brontë

TAO MEANS HOW. THUS, THE TAO OF SLOTH MEANS THE HOW OF SLOTH.
SO HOW WILL YOU SLOTH? HOW WILL YOU NOT SLOTH?

ILLNESS VS. WELLNESS

The only difference between these two words is "I" and "We." Health conscious new-age gurus and motivational-speaking physicians play this word game to illustrate how solely focusing on ourselves can inhibit good health, while focusing on the emotional comfort we receive from other people (and pets) can support us in maintaining good health. What is the first thing you do when you're in need of a hand (or claw)? Do you try to figure things out on your own, or do you ask for help? Do you feel like you can rely on others? If you tend to stick to yourself, yet want to find your tribe, you have to carefully crawl out of your comfort zone and cooperate and connect with other people. You can do it, poky. At the end of their lives, people's biggest regret is that they didn't cultivate closer relationships with their families and friends.

What activities, people, and places
bring you a sense of well-being?
Fill this page with as many
as you can think of.

....
....
....
....
....
....
....
....
....
....
....
....
....
....
....
....
....
....
....
....
....
....

BABY SLOTH STEPS

The cutest babies in all the animal kingdom, baby sloths stick to their moms until they can feed themselves, yet may hang on a little longer, dangling from her for up to four years. How long did it take you to learn to walk, or feed yourself, or tie your shoes? One of the most pervasive premises throughout this book is patience and how to cultivate and exploit this underutilized virtue to your advantage. Think a fully-grown sloth takes small steps for itself? Sloth babies take even smaller sloth steps for sloth kind. We learn best by repetition, which is why you are being encouraged in countless ways to foster tolerance and tenacity in your quest to achieve calm composure in your life, regardless of what goes before you. You can do this best by not biting off more leaf than you can chew (but baby sloths can't fit too much in their tiny mouths to begin with, so, unbutton your top button, slow down, and take it easy).

Take your time finding each item on the list, opposite, then take a photo, print it out, and stick it in the book.

A branch a baby sloth
could wrap its tiny
claws around.

A berry it might try
before deciding it
doesn't like it (don't
you try it either).

A tree you would want
to begin life in if you
were a sloth.

WHAT'S GOOD?

Need an antidote for all that's wrong with the world? We are bombarded with images and stories of negativity and suffering almost everywhere we turn. It's almost too much! Especially for a little creature who just wants to be left alone to live a simple life free from the often overwhelming stresses surrounding the woods where they live. When you find yourself drowning in desperation, depression, or despair simply stop and ask yourself: "What's good?" Expressing your gratitude for everything available and present in your life (inwardly or out loud) dissolves any pressure or fear or uncertainty. You can't experience two diametrically opposed feelings at once (for example, you can't feel pure hate and unconditional love at the same time) and why would you want to? That would just be confusing and frazzle the wires in your little sloth brain.

Make a list of as many things (big or small) you are grateful for.

ACORNS

When was the last time you marveled at the miracle of a majestic oak tree? Or contemplated the proportion of protoplasm to the rest of existence you once were? Size doesn't matter; not to sloths, not to trees, not to human beings, nor to other critters.

Can you even fathom the amount of intelligent quantum specks of information just sitting around like lazy bums in every particle in the known universe? Sloths, like other animals, are blissfully unaware of such thought, and if you truly want to be more sloth-like, perhaps it's best you don't engage in such ruminative theoretical thought.

Sloths limit their mental faculties to a few simple thoughts: Mom, sleep, leaf, bathroom, sleep, repeat. In contrast, deer, red squirrels, chipmunks, wild turkeys, and crows are too busy munching on acorns to concentrate on a second nap. Who has their priorities in order?

WHAT SORT OF POTENTIAL LURKS INSIDE YOU?
FILL THIS SPACE WITH WHAT YOU BELIEVE
YOU ARE CAPABLE OF.

INTERNATIONAL SLOTH DAY

October

20

Every October 20 from now on is already on your calendar, right? If not, go ahead and set the repeat alert to "Never ends." This is one small step you take to honor not only your inner sloth, but also the slight efforts of all the other outer sloths standing (or hanging) up in support of the countless conservation efforts promoting the protection of their special species.

Whether you are a nature- or meme-lover, by now the simple sloth has surely snuggled its way into your heart. Celebrating International Sloth Day with a party in honor of the irresistibly cute and cuddly may become the highlight of your year, perhaps eclipsing even the excitement and anticipation of your own birthday!

Invite your friends, bake a cake, open presents, make a donation to a conservation organization, or even volunteer at a sloth sanctuary for a semester or during your next sabbatical.

List five things you can do to celebrate International Sloth Day.

1

2

3

4

5

BOREDOM

Ever get bummed out when things aren't happening fast enough? Either put this book away (there is no hope for you) or read it again (there is)! You always have options and opportunities, but you don't need to move a muscle if you don't want to.

There will always be more to do, but less time to do it. Invite your inner sloth into your imagination where the grass is always green and it's always 72 degrees Fahrenheit under a blue sky with 50 percent humidity. Remember: By doing nothing, sloths do nothing wrong. Provided you look after yourself, you can relax knowing nothing is your business.

Productivity? Leave that to the mortals on their feet so much they've forgotten to put them up once in a while. Recognition? Fame will only complicate your life. Autographing books, CDs, photos, T-shirts, and posters will get tedious and dull. Best to just let the world pass you by, awash in the intoxicatingly aromatic apathy of boredom.

What do you do now that you could get away with not doing?

MAKE A LIST AND
STICK TO IT.

CREATE
ANYTHING
YOU WANT

You can get what you want even if you move at the speed of sloth. It may take a little longer than if you were a cheetah, but who wants to be a cheetah? They have no idea what a rose smells like (they've never stopped to smell one).

According to the experts, your non-conscious brain doesn't know the difference between something you imagined when your eyes were closed and what happens when they're open. Pretend something you want is already real or has happened and pay attention to how it feels. While in a calm, deep state of relaxation (via deep breathing and/or meditation) re-experience this using as many of your five senses as you can. It takes Herculean focus, but do this every morning, noon, and night for 10 minutes.

Not only will this eventually train your non-conscious mind to believe you can create what you want, you will also begin to see opportunities that align with your new belief that you have what it takes to make it happen.

"IMAGINATION
IS THE BEGINNING
OF CREATION.
YOU IMAGINE
WHAT YOU
DESIRE, YOU
WILL WHAT YOU
IMAGINE, AND AT
LAST YOU CREATE
WHAT YOU WILL."

George Bernard Shaw

JUST LIKE
YOU

There are thousands (maybe even millions) of people who think, feel, and act (and maybe even walk or talk) just like you. You could choose to be a precious and unique snowflake capable of anything you set your mind to or just another slow-moving, do-nothing citizen of the world who no more than warrants an unenergetic "Hi" from your kin (if they even acknowledge you in the first place when you wander your way into their Central and South American jungles hoping to connect with your long-lost relatives).

Unfortunately, being different tends to make people nervous and uneasy (we tend to like people who are like us). So, if you don't seem to find too many slothful tendencies in your nearest and dearest flesh and blood, it's okay to hunt farther afield in search of your clan. Who knows where they are? You have to find them. Make it your mission!

Where in the world do you think your clan are communing?

DO SOME RESEARCH ON YOUR ANCESTORS AND RECORD YOUR FINDINGS HERE.

HI!

HOW TO FACE FEAR

In her book *Comfortable with Uncertainty*, Pema Chödrön asks the question: "Do I grow up and relate to life directly, or do I live in fear?" Living life in the face of all we encounter demands waxing up our surfboards and riding the waves, no matter how quickly they roll in (terrifying to a sloth) or how far from (or near to) shore they break.

What are you scared of? The future? The past coming back to haunt you? "Are you afraid of dying," as Wayne Dyer said, "with your music still in you?" What waves do you want and need to ride? What music do you want and need to play? What do you have to share with the world that only you know how?

When you feel fear frolicking freely into your life and onto your doorstep, instead of closing the drapes, turning off all the lights, and lying down on the floor hoping it will eventually go away, try the friendly approach. Invite it in for tea and a talk. When it asks to sleep over (it always does) politely decline and box up the rest of the cookies as a parting gift. Don't let fear backcomb your coarse fur; wish it well on its way with a smile.

What works when you're scared? What doesn't?

THIS WORKS FOR ME:

THIS DOESN'T:

ENERGY-SAVING MODE

How much energy do sloths consume? Very little (they eat leaves).
Then again, they also expend very little energy. Sloths are in
energy-saving mode 24 hours a day. Do you ever consider how
much energy (and in what forms) you consume and how
you expend it? How much energy do you get from food?
What fuels your car and your house? Do you consciously
conserve or recycle your resources? Why or why not?

It has been estimated that in just six hours, the deserts
on earth receive more solar energy than we consume
in a year. The sun seems like an infinite source of energy,
so why do we rely on (and continue to deplete) non-renewable
sources? One reason is we have invested decades of time, money, and
energy (!) developing the infrastructure to produce, manufacture,
and deliver it. How would a sloth change this?

HOW MUCH ENERGY DO YOU GENERATE A DAY?

NOTHING MATTERS

When you accept things how they are (as sloths seem to do) there is less pressure to conform or perform. When you don't sweat the small stuff and take everything with a grain of salt, you become a walking cliché, but you also end up living like so few do (and are thus happier because you have chosen to).

The reason people struggle so much to slow down is because they're worried they may realize that what they're busy doing doesn't really matter. This author believes we are meant to dance and sing and play, once we've found food and shelter and taken care of others (all else is moot).

If you are frustrated about anything that is not on this TO DO list, re-read this book again. Focus on what's important to you and let the busy bees buzz blindly by in search of who-knows-what (better hang a Do Not Disturb sign on the end of your branch, just in case).

WRITE YOUR
TO-DO LIST
HERE

ABOVE AND BEYOND

According to new research "there's no payoff in going above and beyond the call of duty." This is just what a sloth wants to hear; it justifies their *modus operandi* and absolves them of responsibility for what they didn't (and couldn't) accomplish in the first place (accountability is the last thing on a sloth's mini mind).

Enthusiastic pie-in-the-sky predictions are in danger of not coming to pass, which only leaves shrewd seers shrugging their shoulders wondering what the heck happened (best not to be in the boardroom on their side of the table when the quarterly reports arrive).

To safely go where every sloth has gone before, do your best to neither under-promise nor over-deliver on anything, or else you risk the wrath of the well-intentioned worker bees (uneducated in sloth ways) who will swiftly sully your slothfully-sinful sunny days.

DESCRIBE A TIME YOU KNEW BETTER THAN TO UNDER-PROMISE, AND HAD THE FORESIGHT TO FAR FROM OVER-DELIVER.

HERE ARE SOME SYNONYMS FOR THE WORD "SLOW."

- unhurried
- leisurely
- steady
- relaxed
- chilled out
- delayed
- measured
- sedate
- prolonged